On the Beach

Monica Hughes

OXFORD
UNIVERSITY PRESS

I can see shells on the beach.

I can see pebbles on the beach.

I can see a starfish on the beach.

I can see a crab on the beach.

I can see seaweed on the beach.

I can see seagulls on the beach.

crab

pebble

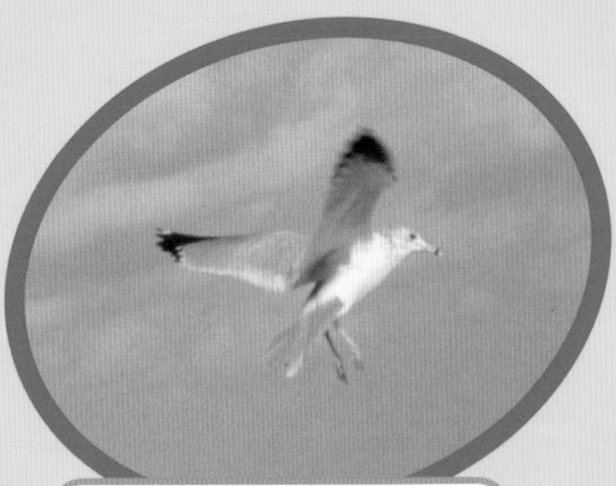
seagull

seaweed

shell

starfish